Childhood Roots

Trail Markers for Raising Children Birth to Eight

Barbara Stacks

Childhood Roots

Trail Markers for Raising Children Birth to Eight

Barbara Stacks

BOOK PUBLISHERS NETWORK
Changing the World One Book at a Time

Book Publishers Network
P.O. Box 2256
Bothell • WA • 98041
Ph • 425-483-3040
www.bookpublishersnetwork.com
<http://www.bookpublishersnetwork.com>

10 9 8 7 6 5 4 3 2 1

Printed in the United States of America

ISBN 978-1-937454-98-2
LCCN 2013946981

Cover design by Carole Day
Illustrations by Sarah Leis
Layout by Karen Desson and Sarah Leis

Dedication

Childhood Roots is a gift for the children, families, and professionals who have guided and inspired my life's work.

Contents

Introduction

*C*hildhood Roots is a guidance book, a teaching text for raising children. It has been written for use with parenting talks. It highlights, but intentionally abbreviates, stages of child development to allow for group discussion. The selected stages, referred to as "Trail Markers," contain well-researched information. Parents will hopefully benefit from repetition, review, and personal validation.

Marshall McLuhan, author, wrote, "The medium is the message." Today's medium, the computer, along with texting, tweeting, clicking, emailing, and googling, rules the day! Digital-age parents move, react, spin with speed, and communicate with few words or slang and imitation. Wow!

Is it time to toss aside society's tech tools and media messages when holding, talking, walking, teaching, and playing with young children? Is it possible to parallel adult gadgetry and parenting experiences? Yes, *Childhood Roots* addresses parenting possibilities. Yes, parenting rules can co-exist with cell phone chatter.

It is quite amazing and often quite impressive that such diversity in parenting styles and child-rearing practices interweave as efficiently as they appear to in the twenty-first century. But are there glitches or gaps that are seriously impacting young children? *Childhood Roots* compares a child's growth cycle with that of a maple tree. Why a tree? And why a maple tree?

The maple tree, and a number of other like trees, produce sap in the early spring. Warm days and cool nights regulate sap production and flow as the environment changes. Tree tappers collect the sap to produce maple syrup. They observe, understand, and respond to the cycles of Mother Nature.

Parenting a child compares nicely with this process. A resourceful parent, having planted the seed, births the child, nurtures the growth, observes the changes, anchors the roots, and produces and creates the child. Just as cells divide and tree rounds form within a tree trunk, so do a child and parent grow with each advancing year. To observe, understand, and cater to a young child's needs, it is necessary—no, vital—to advance slowly with each stage and each round of development.

Fortunately, for both parent and child, child development is adaptive, resilient, and forgiving. Human development is cyclical and predictive. Suckling, babbling, crawling, walking, talking, and so forth, unfold quite naturally. However, digital distraction can put on hold and possibly delete these critical moments. *Childhood Roots* provides for parents "Text Messages" that guide and strengthen the growing-up process.

In the early 1900s, primers were published to teach a child to read. They used the experience and imagination of children to develop vocabulary, rhymes, subject matter, and illustrations to guide the learning process. *Childhood Roots* will provide parents with vocabulary, illustrations, rhymes, and subject matter to guide the parenting process.

Guidance is an optimal word. Trail Markers in *Childhood Roots* are selected guideposts. They serve to strengthen the parenting process. Raising children is complex. Rooms, libraries, warehouses, classrooms, hospitals, DVDs, TV programs, parenting classes, one's own growing-up years, and individual life experiences provide extensive resources and research for child rearing.

Yet, this wealth of information is accessed by a very small percentage of young parents, or it is not accessed at all. I contemplated titling this book, "Spitting in the Wind," precisely because few, if any, young parents will access the information presented in *Childhood Roots*. Nevertheless, I am delighted to share such Trail Markers with young parents. For me, *Childhood Roots* is professional closure.

I know from forty years in the field that a quick fix does not develop the whole child, but rather, relevant and sustaining roots and values early in life strengthen over time. Children grow up, and so do parents! A parent's primary task is to help to develop the inner resources of a child. The early years of childhood are the formative years, the roots. The growing years are dynamic and entwined with parenting. *Childhood Roots* simply offers guidelines and suggestions for patience, perspective, and hope.

Come with me.
Play with me.
Watch the tree grow.
Tap the tree carefully.
See the sap flow.

Child Development

The Whole Child Is

Adaptive

Attentive

Cautious

Confident

Creative

Curious

Educated

Empathetic

Feeling

Giving

Guided

Imaginative

Impressionable

Independent

Intelligent

Investigative

Loving

Nurtured

Parented

Playful

Resilient

Respectful

Secure

Trusting

Vocal

The Whole Child Is Influenced By

Neighborhood and Outside World

Home, Play, and School

Parent Roots and Values

Trail Marker

Nurture

During these early months the baby's general progress in development is largely assured by nature. In terms of having to make choices, it is probably the easiest of all times for parents. If they provide the baby with a normal amount of love, attention and physical care, nature will pretty much take care of the rest.

Burton L. White, 1975
The First Three Years of Life

I am born.
Begin with me.
Take the time to bundle me.
Listen to my breathing sounds.
Bond my life with loving rounds.

Text Message

The first two years of a child's life are critical developmental years. They bond parent and child, and they nurture the roots of trust and confidence. Research studies support these statements.

T. Berry Brazelton, noted pediatrician and development expert, wrote and lobbied for a national two-year child-leave policy in the United States. Such a policy, Brazelton said, would provide parents with employment benefits and time to bond with their offspring during the first two critical attachment and bonding years. Workplaces have been instituting more comprehensive and extended leave practices.

Babies need to attach and bond with caregivers physically and emotionally during these first formative years to survive and to begin to develop lifelong human relationships. Babies are completely dependent on primary caretaking during the first six months of life, attaching to and extending to other caregivers within the second six months. These relationships continue to grow and flourish throughout the second year.

When childcare is provided outside the home (i.e., day-care centers, day-care homes), it is necessary for parents to carefully select centers that are state licensed. Parent surrogates, or replacements, should be well versed in child development. They need to display sensitivity, patience, and warmth, and they will need to employ organizational skills. Infant care is best provided in centers and day-care homes with low staff turnover and infant-caregiver ratios. One consistent adult for two to three infants is optimal in the first year, building to six toddlers in the second year and no more than eight to ten preschoolers in the third to fourth years. High-quality health, nutritional, emotional, and physical standards need to be selected. The State Department of Education licenses childcare facilities and is helpful in providing specific guidelines and information.

Not all parents are emotionally prepared to provide their infants with optimal child nurturance and care. In my experience, I have observed what I refer to as the "nurturance gene." Nurturance is the ability to love, care for, and provide for the needs of others. This ability is quite natural for a large percentage of people. Infants thrive in the arms of nurturance. Infant-care facilities can and do offer the opportunity for young people to observe and to learn nurturing practices.

Young adults, who spend time getting to know each other, set up housekeeping, learn to divide labor and chores, and begin to nurture the home nest. Eventually, adding a pet as a trial run for raising a child might be considered. This advice is not given lightly or facetiously, but rather, routines and a relationship with any animal parallel the human parenting, care-giving, nurturance experience. The adage, "Practice makes perfect," applies. Raising a child is not for everyone, and no one needs to feel guilt or resentment for choosing not to have children.

But should young adults choose to have a child, it is important to understand the nature of attachment and bonding with one's offspring. The cultural shift from home base to workplace is an issue that requires careful and deliberate attention. Avoiding hassle, frustration, anxiety, and stress is the goal!

Nurturing Principle

*T*he first two years of an infant's life are critical developmental years. Adult confidence and interpersonal skills are rooted and anchored during these years. Attaching to and nurturing the needs of one's offspring secure human bonding and lifelong relationships. It is necessary for human infant survival to attach to and bond with primary and secondary care providers during the first year of life and then extending through the second year. Attachment bonds help to give infants nourishment, safety, security, and we hope, nurturance and love.

Parenting Suggestions

Slow down and embrace quiet moments.

Pay close attention to personality and temperament.

Observe more and talk less.

Respect routines and schedules.

Turn off the television and computer.

Put the cell phone away.

Take time to read nursery rhymes and books for young children.

Sing songs and play a wide variety of music.

Hold and rock your baby often. Smile and relax.

Take a deep breath and let it out slowly to relieve anxiety.

Think about and create a quiet, organized home.

Schedule cleaning, cooking, and shopping.

Take frequent walks indoors and outdoors, holding or pushing your baby in a stroller.

Create a quiet environment in your home to help your baby stay calm, focus attention, and receive sensory-motor feedback from you and the environment.

Delay adult gratification, such as shopping, talking on cell phones, running errands, and so forth.

Schedule personal time without your baby. Exercise, talk, and spend time with your spouse, family, and friends. Work on hobbies. Work part-time. Boredom and adult depression occur frequently and can be countered with motivational activities.

Research and choose well-qualified day-care providers and babysitters. Know state guidelines/standards for quality child development practices, day-care centers, etc.

Read about and understand child development.

Seek answers to questions about infant care.

Make mistakes and try again.

Know that birthing a baby results in a job of lifelong nurturance and protection.

Learn about feeding, sleeping, bathing, and protecting practices.

Cherish the early years and know that these years anchor growing roots securely!

Parents as Teachers
Primer Words

Attach	Help
Blanket	Hold
Bond	Nurture
Bundle	Relax
Care	Remember
Caress	Respect
Comfort	Respond
Cradle	Return
Diaper	Rock
Feed	Secure
Handle	Smile

Now I'm growing,
Look at me!
Take the time to nurture me.
Smile, play, go away.
Hurry back and hold me ...

Trail Marker

Trust

With that, Rainbow Fish left the safety of the hiding place. "Let's go!" he called. The other fish trembled with fear, but they knew what they had to do. They sped out of the crack after Rainbow Fish.

Marcus Pfister, 1995
Rainbow Fish to the Rescue

I need to feel your love for me.

Will you come and care for me?

I will look and I will see,

But

Can I trust the roots that

Help anchor me?

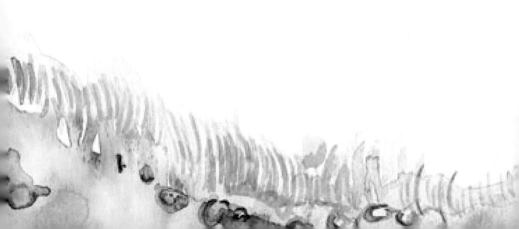

Text Message

Who among us does not understand and search for trust in our lives? How often do we approach or distance people and situations with confidence or anxiety? Handling life with confidence begins early—deep within our childhood roots.

From birth throughout the life cycle, babies, children, and adults possess an inborn need to receive sustenance from the environment. Without sustenance and protection from elements, humans do not survive. This chain of life secures life. Infants and young children learn to expect life-giving protection. Such trust begins at birth with regular and reliable expectation and satisfaction allowing the infant to physically, cognitively, emotionally, and socially begin to develop. Trust and security weave together. A secure, trusting child is free to grow with confidence. The first round of growth spirals to continuing rounds. Confidence walks—no, strides—with bold and steady foot-steps. A small child reaches out, pets the dog … the older child climbs the tree … a young adult boards a plane … and an older adult sleeps peacefully in strange places. Confidence is the ability to handle life with a calm ease. When a baby trusts the world, confidence grows.

A child learns best by imitation. A parent teaches best by dem-onstration. The parenting trick is to trust one's self enough to pass along life lessons acquired over many years. It is extremely difficult to take a well-learned skill and simplify it into individual lessons. For example, an adult dresses quickly each day and has done so for years. Teaching a two-year-old to put on a shirt or a three-year old a jacket or a four-year-old shoes is not easy. But this is the task of raising a child. It is important that a child attempt and accomplish dressing, eating, playing, and so forth in simple, independent steps. It is the parent's job to teach these skills, step back, and encourage mastery. This process takes time, patience, and confidence. Doing for a child what a child is capable of doing communicates a lack of confidence in a child's ability. Adult frustration with a child's lack of skill or with one's own inability to teach a skill undermines confidence in both. A child's self-esteem is intrinsically tied to hard work and accomplishment.

It is important for new parents to try to avoid being easily overwhelmed. Seeking support from one's spouse, family, friends, and other people is truly helpful. It is important to accept who you are and what your bag of skills holds. If you take time to understand a child's age and stage of development, you will know that you need to have trust in your new learned knowledge and yourself. Raising a child occurs over many years, and no one possesses all of the teaching tools or all of the answers. Each baby reveals a unique and a constantly changing set of behaviors. All stages of development share characteristics, but no one guide book or bit of helpful advice will solve all problems. It is okay to make mistakes and feel confident that it is okay. Go ahead, try again! Babies and children are resilient. They will learn and so will you! Value your role as a parent!

Trust Principle

*H*uman species of all ages learn to expect environmental protection. Trust begins at birth, is secured in infancy, and flourishes throughout life. Babies trust parents who respect their daily routines and schedules. They trust parents who come and go with confidence and regularity. They trust parents who trust themselves. Trust is a foundational feeling that supports the beginning of child development. Positive, consistent parenting secures and anchors the roots of life.

Trust is learned, offering all ages a radar screen that monitors security and insecurity, confidence and anxiety. Secure, confident parents raise secure, confident children. Such children seek eye contact, smile comfortably, and reach out their arms with warm expectation. They naturally seek, give, and appear to enjoy novelty. They wait patiently and are confident that the environment will serve their needs—whatever those needs may be.

Babies quickly learn that when they are hungry, they are fed, when they are tired, they will sleep. There is a wonderful rhythm and rhyme in reliability. Babies learn to be cautious and use their radar screens to protect themselves. Babies carefully observe verbal and nonverbal body language. Babies and young children will see and will feel confident actions. They hear calming words and meaningful messages.

Trust and confidence are learned in life. They are foundational feelings that are planted and grow from the interaction of a baby or a child with the environment. Babies and children monitor people and situations with an internal imaging system that potentially offers an inner release from fear and anxiety. Positive and secure interpersonal relationships are anchored in deeply planted roots of reliable nurturance and care. Parents provide protection and reliability.

Parenting Suggestions

Walk, talk, and model skills slowly.

Pay attention to routines and schedules.

Respond with consistency and reliability.

Leave and return frequently.

Monitor your own personal feelings and behaviors and display them appropriately.

Learn how to use positive messages.

Give support and protection without overprotecting and let your child learn by doing.

Step back and allow your child to experience established, as well as novel, experiences.

Be a confident role model. Walk, react, and talk with calm assurance.

Take or read parenting advice and try again with more confidence.

Accept criticism as a way of looking at a problem and not as a personal attack.

Try to relax more, laugh easily, and enjoy experiences.

Make mistakes and understand that this is okay.

Trust your judgment. Your child will trust you.

Parents as Teachers
Primer Words

Attach	Provide
Bond	Relate
Expect	Relax
Give	Satisfy
Nurture	Secure
Organize	Steady
Predict	Supervise
Protect	Sustain
	Trust

Go and come.

Return with ease.

A trusting child yearns to please.

I can stand, and I can walk.

With carefree guidance

I will talk.

I look at you, and all around,

I see the trees that stand

Their ground.

Trail Marker

Play

One of the best ways of ensuring that our children both play and develop lifelong habits of play is to share our personal passions with them. Our passions are activities we love and engage in whenever we have the opportunity to do so. Whether golf, gardening, fishing or jogging, passions give us a creative outlet that we may not find in our jobs or professions. They allow us to realize our personal talents and abilities.

David Elkind, Ph.D., 2007
The Power of Play

I want to play and make-believe,

Hide my eyes, pretend to leave.

When I dress up, play a role,

I forget I'm little; I'm in control!

I stretch the truth.

I problem solve.

Free to think, to roam with ease,

Through many rooms,

I move on knees.

Let me be. Let me play.

I need the time to find my way!

Text Message

A child learns about life through play. Parents and caregivers need to provide sufficient and uncluttered time for children to develop their imaginations. Imagination is an integral part of cognitive development for young children. Imagination is fostered in the young mind with lots of sensory feedback. Contact with clay, water, sand, paints, blocks, moveable toys, dress-up clothes is necessary. In today's digital world, parents often contend that computers, cell phones, and video games are the play materials of childhood. These technological tools are helpful "add-ins" in later childhood, but not in the early childhood years.

A child, from birth to at least age eight, and often beyond, needs to develop interconnections within the brain through problem solving and imagination. Television, the computer, and digital games stimulate and focus eye-hand coordination skills but often fail to integrate and engage the mind in cranial problem solving. A child who develops a high level of imaginative thinking early in life through play, experiences, concentrates, problem solves, and demonstrates better self-control throughout the lifespan.

A child's play world is part of the larger, more integrated world. It is unnecessary for parents to worry about praising play activities. A child needs feedback that recognizes skill, talent, time, work ethic, and uniqueness. All too often, parents provide empty praise that reinforces attention seeking and insecurity. A child's play world is not an end unto itself but, rather, a beginning of the creative process.

A creative child is a thinking, playful child who is curious about life's questions and answers. A creative child wants to discover answers that are obvious and not so obvious. A creative child responds with excitement when the answer to a problem is discovered. When a parent discovers and solves a child's problems, who is more interested in continuing to pursue answers? Childhood is a time for trial and error, and it is okay to distance from one's child to open the door to possibility. Creativity is planted in the garden of childhood and fully matures in adolescence. It is a parent's job to prepare and till the soil that nurtures and grows the most creative ideas, habits, and curiosity of a child. It is the parent's job to provide some assorted play materials. It is the child's job to discover, to create, and to imagine more!

A playing child is absorbed in a world of fantasy, free from rules! Goals exist, but they are designed outside of whatever is being played with or created. A block building becomes an airport, clay becomes a horse or an igloo, a rainbow drawing becomes a bridge from the sky to the earth, and so on. Play is the young child's foundation of intellectual growth, the beginning of cause and effect, the whys of thinking. When a child is given time to play, think, and create, he or she is also learning patience with imperfect solutions and the ability to persist with projects. These playful pastimes quickly become the developing habits for later learning.

Today, free and uninterrupted playtime is quickly becoming erased with academic pressure, overscheduling, and hard-wired technology. Workplace pressure, structured environments, supervision, overprotection, media magic, and time outside are gobbling up a child's developmental need to climb the staircase of creative imagination.

To counter such pressure, it takes developmental education and confidence. It has never been easy for parents to walk away from this debate. Pressure, especially pressure that the media, schools, stores, and even the federal government reinforce, is becoming even more intrusive in the child-rearing arena.

Birth to age eight, however, are exempt years. *Childhood Roots* maintains that these years are growing years that allow for turning off the TV, choosing simple, open-ended playthings, creating an interesting home, and avoiding the temptation to purchase too many toys. Dolls, doll houses, tents, caves, water tubs, modeling clay, storybooks and storytelling, crayons, markers, a work bench, tools, music, fairy tales, puppets, rhymes and rhythms, pots and pans, newspaper piles, and pets to care for are among the BEST play materials for a young child.

Provided with this foundation, quickly and quite naturally after age eight, a child will literally propel off the training trampoline! The eight-year-old is now eager to grab the golden ring of more advanced learning. The eight-year-old is now ready to hold the tech tools of society. The eight-year-old is now ready to climb to higher levels of learning.

Confidence is what all parents need to teach and what young children need to model. A playful parent teaches the value of play! Think about the healing power of play for adults. Play offers a wonderful opportunity to relax and forget the stress of life. Play is learning! A playscape is a child's escape. Play teaches social skills, negotiation, and conflict resolution. These are life skills that require practice and participation with other children. It is important for parents to step aside and provide optimal opportunities for a child to play with other children with minimal adult involvement.

Play Principle

*P*unctuate the purpose and importance of play in your child's development. Avoid mixed media messages that may continue to confuse and complicate the parenting process. Provide playtime for your child that is simple and open to originality.

Children require confident, well-educated parents who provide calm, uncluttered environments where a child is free to create and to problem solve. Concentration is perhaps the most important ingredient of the learning process. It is a parent's responsibility to provide opportunities for concentration to develop in the young mind.

A child's play world is an integral part of cognitive development. Young children require time, materials, and freedom to express their individual abilities. A wise, resourceful parent or caregiver steps back and avoids solving a child's problems. But rather, the early childhood years (birth to eight) are infused with multiple opportunities to explore, to develop, and to express symbolic, abstract aspects of life.

Parenting Suggestions

Sit down and slow down!

Provide time for play activities and experiences.

Provide materials that foster play and imagination (wood, water, sand, clay, dress-up clothes, storybooks, blocks).

Limit and/or ban television and digital gadgetry (cell phones, video games, computers).

Be a confident role model.

When choosing play materials, look for open-ended items that do not solve problems for children (e.g., blocks, Legos, blank paper, not coloring books, puzzles).

Create an uncluttered space in the home where play is fostered.

Be a resourceful parent and provide time and materials for play.

Try not to become an integral part of your child's imaginative play activities.

Step back, observe, be aware, but refrain from doing what your child is capable of doing.

Give positive affirmation by saying, for example, "Your drawing is interesting. Tell me about it … " or "You have worked for a long time this morning. Your buildings are tall … "

Engage in adult play activities for modeling purposes.

Remind yourself often that you are your child's parent and not your child's playmate. Delight in your child's original ideas and creations.

Avoid overpraise and empty, effusive comments, such as, "Your house is great," "Wow, what a super drawing," "I love what you made."

Create opportunities for your child to play with other children and to experience a variety of different play environments.

Provide music, rhymes, rhythm.

Spend time exploring, enjoying, and playing outdoors. Nature is a child's friend, and the world of nature is an interesting play world.

Model adult skills, interests, activities, sports.

Be active, interesting, and playful.

Remember that an adult imagination is not a child's imagination.

Remember that a child's imagination is personal.

Play is purposeful and rewarding for building life skills.

Play lots of games, e.g., card games, board games, make-believe games.

In place of purchasing desired toys, help your child to dream and wish for playthings.

Parents as Teachers
Primer Words

Affirm

Anticipate

Build

Concentrate

Create

Delay

Delight

Dream

Engage

Experience

Fantasize

Focus

Imagine

Interconnect

Limit

Model

Moniter

Observe

Play

Pretend

Provide

Read

Refrain

Research

Role Play

Think

Wish

In my mind, I can see

A moving world, my family.

I like to dream. I want to draw,

Build with blocks, hammer, saw.

Now I thrive. I run. I play,

March, gallop, swing, and slowly sway

Over, through, under tree,

Bend down low, hiding me.

Can you guess what I will be?

No, no, no, you can't see ...

I like to kneel and dig in sand,

Cup and scoop with tiny hand,

Digging deep, far below,

Making tunnels, deep and low.

Sand now shifts, and piles grow high.

Castles climb, point toward sky.

Can you see what comes from me?

No, no, no, you can't see.

Trail Marker

Learn

Just as the twig is bent, the tree's inclined. Common sense suggests that growing organisms are highly adaptive to external influences, but what seemed so apparent to Alexander Pope has caused psychologists to argue bitterly for years. How much is mental ability shaped by environments and how much is in the hands of heredity? After all, the tree still develops bark, leaves, and a functioning root system no matter how the twig gets bent.

Jane M. Healy, Ph.D., 1990
Endangered Minds

I sit, I stare, I smile, I coo,

Looking there, seeing you!

Tiny brain, tucked inside,

Snaps a picture, small, so wide!

Mix and match, bridge and feel,

I learn, I grow, I start to squeal!

When I hear, sing a song,

Close my eyes, not too long,

Tiny brain, tucked inside,

Grows along the tree outside.

Text Message

A baby's brain, a maze with multiple pathways, is wired to exponentially grow with innate, intricate molecular connections. Cognitive development separates humans from other primates in the animal kingdom. Internal brain structures, systems, and external experiences dynamically combine and connect. Processing information, regulating emotion, and instinctively surviving and reacting comprise the brain systems. Stress, anxiety, and helplessness interfere with the operation of these systems. Parents and caregivers need to create an environment that is safe, nurturing, and relaxed for young children. Attachment between mothers and infants, including nursing, vocalizations, maintaining contact, and play are vital components for maintaining healthy child development.

Brain hemispheres contain lobes, four in all: the frontal lobe, the temporal lobe, the parietal lobe, and the occipital lobe. These lobes each have a necessary developmental role. The frontal lobe is the largest lobe. It controls motor function, expressive language, planning, behavior, judgment, direction of attention, and control of impulsivity. The temporal lobe deals with hearing, memory, the comprehension of language, time, and spatial relationships. The parietal lobe processes information with sensory receptors and provides touch, pain, pressure, and temperature feedback. The occipital lobe is the brain center of sight and the processing of visual information. The cerebellum, or the tiny brain, is located in the lower back region of the brain. It controls balance and motor movement. The infant brain is far more complex than these abbreviated facts suggest. They are provided as entry points into the human-brain maze.

To understand and fully appreciate the need for a positive start to life, a very simple text for parents seeking additional information is found in Sources in *Childhood Roots*.

All babies go along the same path in the cycle of life but not with the same tempo. Human development is personal, unique, sequentially staged. To be effective parents, it is necessary to know and understand age and stage characteristics and behaviors. A child cycles through good, bad, calm, and disrupted stages that are influenced by life experiences that occur consistently in a step-by-step climb. The ground plan for growth is predetermined.

From birth through age six, the central nervous system is on fast-forward, exploding in expansive, cognitive, emotional, and physical growth. The baby enters an exciting and magical forest of problem solving and imagination. It is important to observe that a child's intellectual ability expands or is limited by make-believe and experimentation with the natural world. Talking, pretending, fantasizing, using language, exploring, and learning how the world works are normal and necessary problem-solving skills. The wise parent will provide outlets and time for these skills to mature. A child who has multiple opportunities to manipulate sounds and sensory-motor experiences will have more success reading, writing, and using symbols after age six.

A baby's brain is a multiple-pathway maze that is wired to exponentially and innately grow to form molecular connections. Cognitive development, however, combines inborn structure and systems with external experiences. Processing information, feeling emotions, and instinctually surviving comprise the brain.

Attachment between mother and infant, through nursing, vocalizing, and contact, help to strengthen cognitive, emotional, reactive, and social development. A baby's brain receives, stores, and retrieves information instantaneously. It is the parent's job to filter the baby's world. Overstimulation and understimulation clutter and declutter the brain's storehouse. Balance is the primary goal of parenting!

Between the ages of five and eight years, a child's brain is dynamically changing. More important, the young brain needs to consolidate what has already been learned. Repetition is how a child learns best in order to layer new information.

Learning Principle

*T*he brain is multilayered, multifaceted and intricately connected. Processing information, ruling emotion, and reacting are instinctual and grow systematically. The brain separates human development from other primates. The brain is the power engine of cognitive development allowing an infant and child to learn and progress through unique and unevenly timed ages and stages. Brain development is malleable and requires protection. It is an adult's responsibility to supervise a child's play activities. Falling and injuring the frontal lobe of the brain may not initially appear to cause serious or subtle brain damage. However, soft signs of learning difficulties are often the result of childhood accidents. A child's brain is a magical castle, surrounded by a moat of fluid brimming with creative potential!

Parenting Suggestions

Slow down and observe changes!

Learn about brain development.

Understand ages and stages of child development.

Provide multiple opportunities for infant exploration and child play.

Interact, talk, play, and read often.

Create an interesting home to stimulate problem-solving behaviors.

Monitor and avoid activities that may harm the brain.

Combine sensory experiences (water, sand, clay, paints, crayons, etc.) with motor activities (balancing, crawling, climbing, swinging, swimming, digging, cycling, galloping).

Be a positive role model. Speak slowly but naturally with good vocabulary.

Be patient and allow child the sufficient time to respond using his or her developing sounds and vocabulary.

Smile often. Be silly and playful.

Lead, rather than judge, correct, or punish. Take a breath, step back, observe, listen, and try again.

Repeat information. Baby says, "Book," and you say, "Yes, book." Be specific!

Feel comfortable making mistakes. It is human, normal, and necessary.

Know that the tiny brain that you see is multilayered and multiwired to receive and store much more than it can show.

Feed the brain with sensory stimulation but not with overstimulation.

Parents as Teachers
Primer Words

Attach	Play
Balance	Predict
Connect	Pretend
De-stress	Problem Solve
Experiment	Question
Explore	Read
Fantasize	Role Play
Feel	See
Hear	Smell
Imagine	Speak
Intuit	Stimulate
Learn	Talk
Nurture	Taste

Think

When I shut my eyes at night,

I close the door; I shut off sight.

I breathe the air; I hear the sound,

My brain, it sleeps, swirls around.

Tomorrow is another day

To learn, to think, to see, to play.

Trail Marker

Communicate

Whether you consider that language is a gift from the hi-erarchies or from the mechanics who created the wiring in the brain, it must still have models in order to develop. So talk to and with your child a lot! Most people would guess that we have language because we can think but it appears more accurate to say that we are able to think because we have language.

Rahima Baldwin Dancy, 1989
You Are Your Child's First Teacher

Hear me giggle. Hold me tight.

Play with me, sheer delight!

Hand-in-hand, we walk along.

Birds in trees, hear their song.

Hide your eyes. Count one, two, three!

Can you find me past the tree?

Now sit down; pick up a stick.

Draw a circle with the tip.

Let's walk some more, hand-in-hand,

Pretend we're in a marching band.

Now it's time to turn around,

Hand-in-hand, without a sound.

Down the path, you walk. I run

Behind the trees, we see the sun.

You talk to me and hear me say,

"Come on, Daddy. Want to play?"

Hear me giggle. Hold me tight.

Read to me. Say, "Good night."

Text Message

*A*ll animals communicate with movement, response, and sounds. But, unlike any others in the animal kingdom, humans, through high-level brain development, speak with words.

Learning to use language and to communicate are basic to child development. From birth, babies respond to the human voice. They listen to words, sentences, stories and, through imitation, begin to coo and babble sounds. Language pathways connect in the brain and emerge at different rates. Initially, a baby comprehends more information than he or she speaks. By age one, babies are normally able to say individual words, and by eighteen months to two years, they combine words into phrases, and eventually they speak sentences.

There are such tremendous differences in language production that, all too often, social pressure regarding the baby talking can increase anxiety in parenting. Some babies babble a lot and other babies observe a lot. Some babies talk early, and other babies talk quite late. Yet, babies of different ages are developing within normal guidelines. Usually when a baby begins to walk, he or she will also begin to say some words and combine sounds that imitate parent prompters, i.e., ma ma, da da, etc. The important messages here are that language will emerge and communication is important. Verbal language, including crying, directly begins to build an interactive bond between parent and child. However, nonverbal language is also a necessary communication skill.

Edward Hallowell, M.D., in *The Childhood Roots of Adult Happiness,* expresses this thought quite well. "Touch, hug, snuggle, kiss, pat, wrestle, roll ... I urge you to use physical touch as much as you can. Physical coziness in a family is one of life's greatest pleasures ... You can't ignore a hug." Nonverbal engaging, or social interaction, is communication. A baby or a child who experiences interaction with the world begins to comprehend life's messages and is more alert to language and its link to life. A baby will observe, mouth a word, and pay close attention to the emerging sound. These words, these sounds, are the cambium layers of cognitive growth, the growing rings of language. A talking timetable is not definitive, but there are developmental guidelines to understand.

Birth to Age Two

A baby vocally experiments, imitates sounds, strings sounds, speaks words, mimics, recognizes, and remembers missing objects, people, phrases, short sentences, produces baby talk.

Age Two to Eight

This is a stage of rapid vocabulary growth. More complex sentence development and comprehension of language develop. Questions, questions, and more questions pop up. Language repeats. Self-talk and the recognition of auditory and visual sounds and symbols occur. A child begins to rhyme, combine sounds, and sequence information. A child begins to think and to tell stories that grow in detail and length. A wise parent writes down the words of the child as he or she speaks and repeats these simple stories for the child to hear and enjoy.

Social interaction skills also begin to develop and grow in the early childhood years. These social skills expand communication. Engaging first with primary and secondary caregivers initiates the social spiral. Play, for the child, creates interactive opportunities with adults, other infants, children, and imaginary playmates. Adults have a responsibility to find multiple moments to react, respond, talk, and play with a child. Beyond the home and neighborhood, playgroups, day care, and preschools offer additional play experiences with other children. These experiences are communication opportunities.

A child needs to learn how to handle different feelings, situations, behaviors, and people. Aside from interacting with unique and diverse temperaments and personalities, a child needs to practice communicating. A child, upon entering formal schooling, fares best when he or she is able to communicate with adults and peers effectively. Clear speech is a significant precursor and positive boost to social interaction, as well as learning to read and write symbolic information. Speech production is a motor, as well as a sensory, skill. These sensory-motor abilities develop differently in boy and girl babies. The nervous system of a girl develops by age two, whereas a boy, by age four. Language and sensory-motor skills form the foundation for learning.

There is still another developmental aspect of language that all too frequently is misunderstood and possibly eliminated from parent education. Daniel Goleman refers to the "roots of empathy" in his book *Emotional Intelligence*. Goleman defines empathy as "the ability to know how another feels ... the key to intuiting another's feelings is in the ability to read nonverbal channels: tone of voice, gesture, facial expression and the like." Child-parent communication is cradled with empathetic, nonverbal language. How a parent speaks and conveys information is just as important as the spoken words. In fact, often the tone and nonverbal body language speak more loudly. Awareness of body language and nonverbal messaging needs to be recognized as vital to the challenge of parenting. A child learns to respect and show kindness to others when parented with positive role models. Parents who take multiple opportunities to teach empathy toward family members, playmates, strangers, and animals help their child to grow into trees without broken branches. Communication skills, verbal and nonverbal, are the foundation of positive human care.

Communication Principle

Verbal and nonverbal communication conveys feeling and cognition. Listening, comprehending, responding, and speaking significantly enhance the mental abilities and social interaction skills of the young child. Interpersonal development begins in childhood through communication. It is a wise, well-educated parent who takes time to listen to, think about, and speak with short, clear, and specific sentences when communicating with a child. Reflective listening is a profound communication skill. If a child speaks sentences that describe what is happening in and out of his or her thoughts, a wise, intuitive parent will decipher what the child is talking about and reflect or mirror what has been said. A baby babbles, and a parent knows that the baby is responding to a moving mobile of dancing balls. "You like to look at moving balls." A child may talk about a turtle in the pond, and as a parent you say, "The turtle is swimming in the pond." These are wonderful opportunities to repeat your child's words and thoughts and to extend language!

Parenting Suggestions

Slow down and speak slowly and softly.

Hold, touch, and interact with your infant or your child. Smile often!

Read books and sing songs that use color, rhyme, and repetition.

Speak slowly and clearly and use a variety of tone and intonation.

Pronounce words carefully so that your baby or your child hears the enunciation of sound.

Avoid excess baby talk.

Be an adult role model for language acquisition.

Limit how much you say to allow response time from your child.

Avoid the use of cell phones and gadgetry when communicating.

Use eye contact when mouthing sounds and words.

Remember that nonverbal gestures and nonverbal behaviors (such as hugging) are just as important as verbal language.

Show and teach empathy with verbal and nonverbal responses (such as, "The baby is crying," or "The baby is sad").

Use child literature as a source for teaching feelings, behaviors, and problem solving.

Teach and model communication skills.

Practice listening skills.

Parents as Teachers
Primer Words

Develop	Look
Empathize	Mouth
Encourage	Move
Engage	Prompt
Feel	Question
Hear	Read
Hold	Repeat
Interact	Say
Label	Sign
Laugh	Speak
Learn	Talk
Listen	Write

Do you hear the words I speak?

Baby bird moves its beak.

Sounds I hear, words I say,

These words, they grow day by day.

The world is big. I do not know

Just how big my mind will grow.

Trail Marker

Guide

There should never be any question about who's running the family circus. It is the child's inalienable right to be informed early in life that parents are the ringmasters ... Parents cannot effectively communicate their love to a child unless they are also a source of effective authority.

John Rosemond, 1994
Daily Guide to Parenting

Take my hand; hold it tight.

Help me learn wrong from right.

Touch my tender, growing roots,

Seeds of life, spreading shoots.

Are you the tree that gives the tap,

From which I taste the sugar sap?

I will walk from tree to tree,

Mark the trail, just for me.

Up above my tiny head,

Spread the branches, leaves they shed.

Deep within the tree they feed,

Making sap from tiny seed.

Swirl, then pile,

Begin to fall.

Guide, stand straight,

Oh so tall!

Take my hand; hold it tight.

I need to learn you're out of sight.

Leaves they fall all around.

I walk, I run

On covered ground.

Text Message

A child takes a crayon and draws a stick figure on a piece of paper. Putting the crayon down, the child chooses a second crayon and, bottom up, draws a tall tree on either side of the stick figure. Putting the crayon down, the child chooses a third crayon and draws a large sun on the top of the paper. Putting the crayon down, the child takes the first crayon and draws four block letters across the bottom of the paper.

The stick figure is the child. The trees are the parents. The sun is warm feelings for the family, and the letters are the child's name. Tall trees, tall buildings, animals, and block letters are frequently drawn by children to symbolically show meaningful relationships in their lives.

John Rosemond, noted parent educator, refers to this framework in his book *Parent Power*: "Children learn the value of independence, not as something to be taken for granted, but something to be worked for, and therefore something worth taking care of. You [the parent] are the boss. Talk trees!"

For decades, child development specialists, doctors, and educators have researched and stressed the need for a child to be nurtured, raised, and parented within a stable family. The boundaries that parents provide separate a child from the marriage, the relationship rounds of the tall trees.

The cover of *Childhood Roots* shows a child tasting tree sap from a maple tree. Learning to walk from Trail Marker to Trail Marker, to stop and taste or to run or avoid, is a child's journey through life. Parents, however, mark the path.

Tree taps are normally quite tight, secure, and protective. Raising a child, like tapping a tree for the production of maple syrup, requires skill, time, consistency, and protection. A combination of simple, routine practices and scientific knowledge is necessary. Raising children, like tapping trees, is time-honored. The process should not pose difficulty, but often it does.

Throughout the world, children differ in color, race, language, size, and shape. Parenting practices vary widely. Regardless, all children unfold, develop, and grow according to human timetables. They crawl, stand up, babble, read, and write. Today, more and more comparative research is concluding that American parenting practices are raising children in conflict. Why is this conflict occurring? There is confusion in our fast-paced, rapidly developing nation. Time-tested parenting practices are being inconsistently replaced with clever and motivating media messages that rely less on child development research and more on product marketing and advertising. Americans, these studies conclude, are "collectively infatuated" with their children, with themselves, and with their appearances and possessions, while at the same time, challenged and confused with successful parenting practices. Yes, babies, toddlers, and preschoolers are delightful to watch and fun to play with, as well as difficult to teach and manage effectively. Listening to and directing a child while talking on a cell phone are incompatible.

Human behavior, good and not so good, is easily reinforced. For example, attention-seeking behavior is a major motivating need of a child that can also become a parenting stumbling block, a robust root that pushes up and out of the earth. Other needs to consider are survival, security, affection, and self-esteem. And still beyond these necessary basic life requirements are the needs for justice, beauty, order, and goodness.

A child wants and needs approval. A child wants to please. To satisfy these needs, a parent who loves a child and wants to raise a secure, cooperative, and capable child cannot simply love the child but also needs to be a responsible and creative trail guide!

A parent's job is to problem solve each behavior and each and every situation. Resourceful parents follow the steps of logical problem solving to solve child-rearing problems. They OBSERVE what is happening, THINK of ways to address the problem, ACT with direct action, and finally EVALUATE whether or not the action has worked. Then, they REWARD and REINFORCE, e.g., "Thank you for putting your trucks on the shelf." Use specific words rather than more general directions, such as, "Put your toys away."

A child will cry, whine, or have a temper tantrum when unable to get what he or she desires. A parent needs to assess carefully why the child is reacting this way. Is the child hungry, tired, frustrated, or unhappy? A parent needs to step back, calmly find a solution, and many times, walk away. A common parenting mistake is to show excessive emotion and talk too much. A child does not need reasons for good behavior and misbehavior. The less talk a parent provides, the more readily a child will realize that his or her actions are not that important.

Parent talk is very helpful when teaching new skills or the whys and hows of new information. Parent talk is not helpful when limiting a child's behavior. Actions speak louder than words.

Rules, consequences, and limits need to be clear, easily stated, and understood. Holding a child's hand, acknowledging feelings, establishing eye contact, avoiding problems, supervising, noticing and paying attention to positive behavior, and referring to a short list of rewards and consequences truly help to communicate love and confidence.

Love is the foundation of limit setting. A resilient and well-parented child is also a calm child with positive self-esteem that has been earned. The following parenting suggestions are the result of time-honored research.

Guiding Principle

*P*arents are the teachers and role models for their children. They teach children to be self-disciplined. They provide love and nurturance with limits and boundaries within which children learn. Parents are primary problem solvers who carefully gather information to guide their parenting practices. Confident parents observe and actively listen to their children. They follow through with consistency.

Parents, as teachers, model excellent adult communication skills. They listen more than speak. They use simple, declarative sentences. They avoid questions when directing a child's behavior. Parents use positive and descriptive statements. Parents try not to do for a child what a child is developmentally able to do for himself or herself.

Parents as Teachers
How to Guide and Develop Self-esteem

Be a parent who actively problem solves situations and raises a child who becomes an active problem solver.

Be positive and trust that your child will be positive.

Respond to positive attention-seeking behavior.

Ignore negative attention-seeking behavior.

Reward positive temperament characteristics (active, affectionate, cuddly, good-natured, etc.).

Respect an independent child.

Reinforce a child's social interactive skills.

Enjoy a comfortable, trusting child who plays vigorously, is self-reliant, seeks novel experiences, and is able to ask for help.

Reinforce a trusting child who is comfortable with children and older people.

Provide for hobbies and creative interests. Be a resource, not a playmate.

Maintain a sense of humor.

Make sure that your child has a close bond with at least one family member.

Carefully seek surrogate caregivers.

Participate in steady and gainful full-time or part-time employment.

Structure rules and assign chores in the home.

Maintain a balanced lifestyle.

Make sure your child is well liked by other children and has at least one, and usually more, close friends.

Focus on your child's individual strengths.

Be a role model who listens more, talks less, and participates in individual pursuits.

Choose teachers who are skillful in teaching, are warm and caring, supervise effectively, are well organized, and are knowledgeable in child development.

Reward helpfulness and cooperation.

Help your child develop a talent, interest, hobby, or activity that your child receives pleasure from.

Guide your child to reach out to others and perform acts of kindness.

Spend time with your child, especially if you are employed outside the home.

Teach your child how to save and how to spend money.

Carefully choose play groups, preschools, and neighborhoods.

Choose schools with low child-to-adult ratios.

Avoid pressuring your child to read, write, and do math too soon. Learning is not a race!

Read to and with your child often and regularly.

Go to libraries and read children's literature to teach life lessons and coping skills.

Put aside eBooks, texting, cell phones, and computers as child-rearing gadgetry during these early years. Use them independently without your child.

Encourage your child to play alone, create, and pretend.

Teach right and wrong.

Correct misbehavior.

Avoid organized sports and/or activities that may possibly injure your child's brain.

Try not to overprotect, overfocus, or overindulge.

Teach good manners.

Seek help or advice when in doubt.

Introduce your baby or child to stores, restaurants, and other homes slowly and with careful training. These outings need to be considered "field trips with rules." Each setting has a specific purpose, which the child needs to understand prior to the outing. These settings are not playgrounds.

Model adult communication skills and avoid the use of slang.

Respect and provide quiet time each and every day.

Understand and maintain good nutritional habits.

Understand and maintain age-appropriate sleep routines.

Know that a young child requires to be fed and to go to bed early and at consistent times.

Basic reading, writing, and math instruction is both homework and school work.

For the first four years, a child needs multiple sensory experiences, e.g., fingerpaints, water, sand, markers and crayons, scissors, puzzles, mazes, chalk, etc. Large pencils, crayons, markers, and chalk are initially held with a "fist grasp" and later will transition to a "finger grasp."

Know that boys develop their fine motor skills more slowly than girls. A percentage of boys may require additional time prior to formal school entrance to speak, pronounce, and draw letters.

A child should enter school speaking clearly. At four and five years, a child should be able to pronounce letter sounds and, prior to reading, combine two sounds and begin to recognize frequently used words and directions. Name letters and other letters are frequently practiced during the fifth year. Practice by the child with a parent precedes school practice.

Be a confident, well-educated parent who observes your child and makes decisions and adjustments, based on individual, not social, demands. Consider whether or not your child should enter formal school programs or alternative programs during these formative developmental years.

Be playful, play simple games, problem solve.

Continue to pursue adult activities, education, and employment.

Focus on "Grandma Rules!" Listen more and talk less.

Maintain "child free" time within your marriage.

Parents as Teachers
Primer Words

Choose	Play
Laugh	Practice
Listen	Read
Love	Research
Model	Select
Nurture	Speak
Observe	Stimulate

Teach

Through the woods, trees so dear,

I walk the path, feel no fear.

In and out, I go with ease,

Practicing "yes," "hello," and "please."

I see the signs, say the sounds,

Count the twigs, make the rounds.

Where I start, where I go,

Trees will guide me, I will know.

I can wander now alone,

Let go your hand,

Practice skills you give, I've honed.

Trail Marker

Let Go

All life events are formative. All contribute to what we become, year by year, as we go on growing. As my friend the poet Kenneth Koch once said, "You aren't just the age you are. You are all the ages you ever have been!"

Fred Rogers, 2004
*The World According
to Mister Rogers*

When the sap stops its flow,

Little child will pause, will go.

Through the woods, along the way,

Trees stand tall. Hear them say,

"Roots were planted far below

Solid ground from which they grow.

You tapped the tree, sucked the sap,

Climbed the trunk, let go the tap.

Can you find the way to go

When the sap stops its flow?"

Text Message

*L*etting go is a parenting priority, a preparation process ... boot camp for life. When a child begins to walk, the parent lets go; when a child balances on a two-wheel bicycle, the parent lets go; and when a child climbs onto the school bus, the parent lets go. The primary goal of secure, confident parenting is letting go, letting the child grow into a mature, responsible, unique individual. It is the parent's job to allow this process to unfold with as little anxiety as possible.

When children have acquired skills, they feel capable. They believe in themselves. They have practiced tip-toeing, walking, and running on logs. You, the parents, have guided the walk in the woods using timely and valuable trail markers along the way. You have provided multiple learning opportunities for your child to acquire confidence. Your child has held onto you, trusted you, listened to and talked with you, played and problem solved, learned numbering and ABCs.

It is now time to let go, to walk away. A capable, resilient child is a happy child, raised with love and respect. Raising a resilient child requires trust in the parenting process. Allowing a child to do what he or she is capable of doing conveys trust, even when a child falls down, commits an error, makes a mistake. To learn competence requires practice.

A capable, resilient parent calmly and quietly trusts the process and understands the parenting role. John Rosemond punctuates the three *C*'s of good communication with a child:

Be commanding, as opposed to demanding.

Be concise, as opposed to long-winded.

Be concrete, as opposed to obscure.

Then, walk away, let go! A child intuitively understands parenting words. A child with average intelligence does not require word explanations and definitions. There is a time to speak and a time not to speak. Your child will figure it out!

Adults have spent a lifetime learning the whys and hows of information. It is tempting to fill in a child's blank stares and empty sentences. It is the wise parent who listens attentively, observes from afar, and waits patiently for questions and answers. This is the essence of respect as a parent and as a receiving child.

Trail Marker One of *Childhood Roots* discusses the attachment principle—the critical stage of bonding with one's baby. Letting go is, quite literally, the severing of this attachment in order for the child to survive without the parent. When a child enters formal schooling, he or she should be able to put into motion necessary learning skills. Parenting and letting go of children are a process. It does not happen in a day or a year, but within a lifetime. Patience, practice, and purpose form a framework, a strong set of trees. Trees take years to secure roots, grow branches, and develop rings of growth. So, too, do children need time to develop and grow in confidence.

Letting Go Principle

*L*etting go is a parenting paradigm, a child's rite of passage. It requires confidence and trust allowing a child to go forward and upward with stability. Letting go is the separation of child and parent. It is a critical stage of development.

To develop and grow into a unique, independent, and competent person, a child has walked along the path of early childhood. Parents have nurtured the roots, and the Trail Markers have guided the way. Now is the time for the trees to stand tall and straight. The child now lets go and walks away.

Parents as Teachers
Primer Words

Allow	Prepare
Command	Process
Distance	Provide
Free	Respond
Learn	Secure
Let Go	Simplify
Mature	Strengthen
Observe	Trust

Now I'm free to go alone,

cross a stream, kick a stone.

In my brain and in my heart,

I know when to stop, where to start.

You gave to me many tools,

Many lessons, many rules.

Which of these will I keep or lose?

How will I decide which to choose?

Talk to me. Hold me tight.

Turn off the light.

Say, "Good night!"

Spread Roots

Health

Intelligence

Judgment

Empathy

Autonomy

Creativity

Friendship

Nurturance

Love

Those who believe in our ability do more than stimulate us. They create for us an atmosphere in which it becomes easier for us to succeed.

John H. Spalding, author

Fast Forward ... Looking Back

*F*or every suggestion presented in *Childhood Roots,* there will be an exception, a unique situation, and probably many more suggestions will arise. This is the challenge of raising children!

I am hopeful, however, that *Childhood Roots* has motivated you to think about the importance of your parenting role. The examples you set and the values you share with your children will make a profound difference in their future and a feeling of accomplishment in you.

Nurture

Trust

Play

Learn

Communicate

Guide

Let Go

Spread Roots

These are the Trail Markers for a happy, productive life.

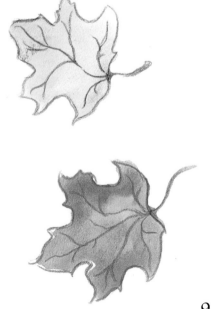

98

Sources

Bluestein, Jane, and Lynn Collins-Fantozzi. *Parents in a Pressure Cooker.* New York: ISS Publications, 1985.

Bowlby, John. *Maternal Care and Mental Health.* Geneva: World Health Organization, 1951.

Brazelton, T. Berry, and Joshua D. Sparrow. *Touchpoints Three to Six.* Cambridge, MA: Perseus Publishing, 2001.

Brooks, Robert, and Sam Goldstein. *Nurturing Resilience in Our Children.* New York: Contemporary Books, 2003.

Conyers, Marcus, and Lola Heverly. *BrainSMART, Early Start: Building the Brain Power of Young Children.* Winter Park, FL: BrainSMART, 1999.

Crary, Elizabeth. *Love & Limits.* Seattle, WA: Parenting Press, Inc., 1994.

———. *Help! The Kids Are at it Again.* Seattle, WA: Parenting Press, Inc., 1997.

Dancy, Rahima Baldwin. *You Are Your Child's First Teacher*. Berkeley, CA: Celestial Arts, 2000.

Elkind, David. *The Hurried Child*. Reading, MA: Addison-Wesley Publishing Company, 1981.

———. *The Power of Play*. Cambridge, MA: DaCapo Lifelong Books (Perseus Books Group), 2007.

Gardner, Howard. *Multiple Intelligences*. New York: BasicBooks, 1993.

Gesell, Arnold, Frances Ilg, and Louise Bates Ames. *Infant & Child in the Culture of Today*. New York: Harper & Row Publishers, 1974.

Goleman, Daniel. *Emotional Intelligence*. New York: Bantam Books, 1995.

Greenwood, C. R., Dale Walker, Judith Carta, and Susan Higgins. "Cognitive Abilities of Children 1–4 Years Old: The Early Problem Solving Indicator." *School Psychology Review*, 35 (4), 535-551, 2006.

Hallowell, Edward M. *The Childhood Roots of Adult Happiness*. New York: Ballantine Books, 2002.

Healy, Jane M. *Endangered Minds*. New York: Simon & Schuster, 1990.

Heath, Harriet. *Using Your Values to Raise Your Child to Be an Adult You Admire*. Seattle, WA: Parenting Press, 2000.

Johnson, Spencer. *The One Minute Mother*. New York: William Morrow and Company, Inc., 1983.

Maxwell, John C., and Jim Dornan. *Becoming a Person of Influence: How to Positively Impact the Lives of Others*. Nashville, TN: Thomas Nelson, Inc., 1997.

Pfister, Marcus. *Rainbow Fish to the Rescue!* New York: North-South Books, 1995.

Rogers, Fred. *The World According to Mister Rogers*. New York: Hyperion, 2004.

Rosemond, John. *Daily Guide to Parenting*. Grantsburg, WI: Sta-Kris, Inc., 1994.

———. *Parent Power!* Kansas City, MO: Andrews and McMeel, 1990.

Rubin, Zick. *Children's Friendships*. Cambridge, MA: Harvard University Press, 1980.

Schaefer, Charles E., and Theresa Foy DiGeronimo. *Ages & Stages*. New York: John Wiley & Sons, Inc., 2000.

Walker, C. Eugene, and Michael C. Roberts, eds. *Handbook of Clinical Child Psychology*. Second ed. New York: John Wiley & Sons, Inc., 1992.

White, Burton L. *The First Three Years of Life*. New Jersey: Prentice-Hall, Inc., 1975.

Zim, Herbert, and Alexander Martin. *Trees, A Guide to Familiar American Trees*. New York: St. Martin's Press, 2001.

Acknowledgments

*C*hildhood Roots has developed over time. It offers a combination of research, experience, and book-bound guidance for parenting. The positive nurturance and guidance of young children will always be the foundation of a future stable society.

Thank you family, friends, and colleagues: Sophie Marsh for her lettering and design background but most especially her warmth and encouragement; Katie Balocca for her ability to combine text with color design and for her patience, support, suggestions, and friendship throughout the book-publishing journey; June Akers Seese, a published author and soul mate, who by example has encouraged me to proceed forward and provide for young families a mentoring model; Karen Desson for her ability to proofread and edit *Childhood Roots*. Karen has been a longtime friend. I am profoundly grateful for her friendship, professional talent, and her enduring encouragement. Thank you.

About the Author

*B*arbara Stacks, teacher, psychologist, counselor, play therapist, speaker, and parent coach has worked with, played with, and researched young children for over forty years. Her work has spanned both private and public school settings. She developed and directed a private preschool as a prototype for developmental readiness in Windsor, Connecticut. In 1994, she established a private practice, Child Guidance Services, in Simsbury, Connecticut. She has authored numerous publications and received notable awards.

Barbara has the ability to motivate and direct change. *Childhood Roots* combines research and experience with young children. The poems that frame each section are original. They were created as memories of magical moments spent with children.

Barbara has retired but continues to speak, facilitate parenting workshops, and preside at national conferences. She resides with her husband in Essex, Connecticut.

About the Illustrator

Sarah Leis is an illustrator, graphic designer, and fine artist. She practices in many mediums, but especially enjoys creating whimsical watercolor illustrations for children's books. Sarah's work has been published in *Another Bird in the Nest* by Lisa Figel and *Honey, Because* by Jeff Gibson. She most recently studied at the Lyme Academy College of Fine Art in Old Lyme, Connecticut. One of her oil paintings was shown at the Copley Society of Boston in 2012. Sarah currently teaches art and design courses at the University of Central Oklahoma. She lives in Oklahoma City with her partner, Cameron, and their beagle, Billy.

About the Cover Artist

*T*he watercolor used for the cover of *Childhood Roots* was painted by Carole Day in 1979. The child is the author's daughter. She is peeking into a sap bucket. Her dad tapped maple trees to teach the natural sugaring cycle that occurs each spring.

Carole paints in *plein air* as well as in her home studio in North Granby, Connecticut. She has studied locally with many artists, is a juried member of several professional affiliations, and is an active member of the Avon Arts Association and West Hartford Art League in Connecticut. Carole has won Awards of Excellence, Best-in-Show Awards and Featured Artist Awards.